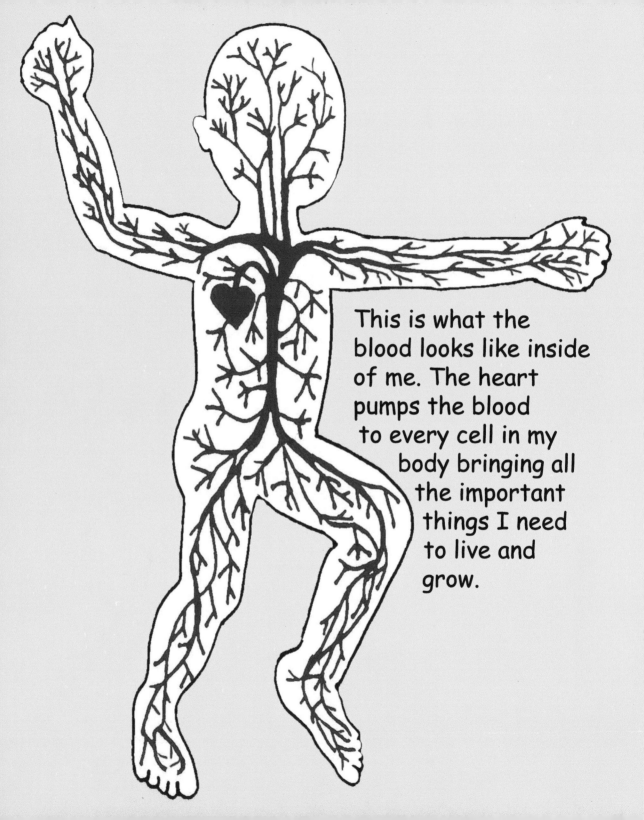

This is what the blood looks like inside of me. The heart pumps the blood to every cell in my body bringing all the important things I need to live and grow.

Chemo to the Rescue

A Children's Book About Leukemia

My House

Me

by
Mary Brent
and Caitlin
Knutsson

BLUE

My Dog

AuthorHouse™
1663 Liberty Drive, Suite 200
Bloomington, IN 47403
www.authorhouse.com
Phone: 1-800-839-8640

First published by AuthorHouse   10/21/2008

ISBN: 978-1-4343-9720-1 (sc)

Printed in the United States of America
Bloomington, Indiana

This book is printed on acid-free paper.

authorHOUSE®

WHAT IS BLOOD?

The blood is made up of millions of tiny cells. These cells travel in a liquid called plasma through large and small tubes called veins and arteries. Notice that there are not only red blood cells. Do you see any other colors?

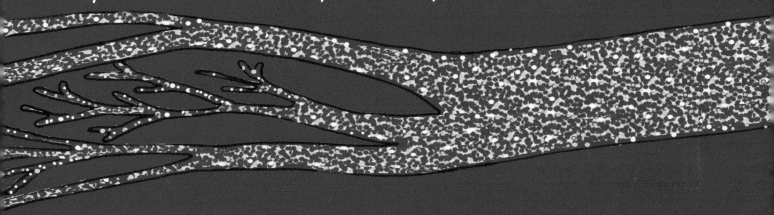

WHERE IS THE BLOOD MADE?

The blood cells are made in the bone marrow. The bone marrow is a soft and spongy tissue found inside the bones. The bone marrow can make as many as five billion blood cells a day.

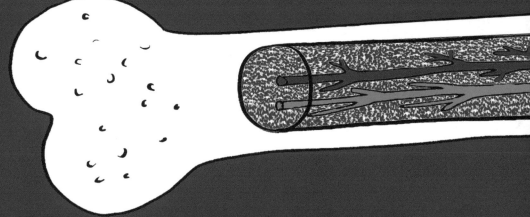

If Dr. Dan puts a drop of blood under the microscope;
he can see these tiny blood cells very big. He can see red
blood cells, white blood cells, and platelets. All three of
these cells do some very important things for your body.

RED CELLS

The red blood cells carry the oxygen from the air that I breathe to every cell in my body.

WHITE CELLS

The white cells eat all the bad germs in my body that can make me sick.

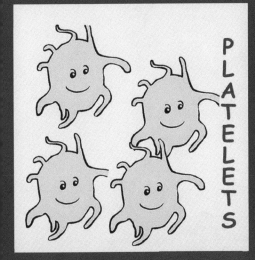

PLATELETS

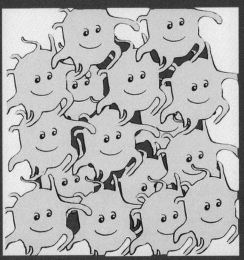

The platelets repair cuts. They clump together to form a scab, which stops the bleeding.

LEUKEMIA

BUT, WHAT WERE THESE ODD LOOKING CELLS DOING IN MY BLOOD?

They shouldn't be there! These were NOT hard working cells. They could NOT eat the germs in my body. They lived too long in my blood doing absolutely nothing but take up space. Dr. Dan said it was called "leukemia".

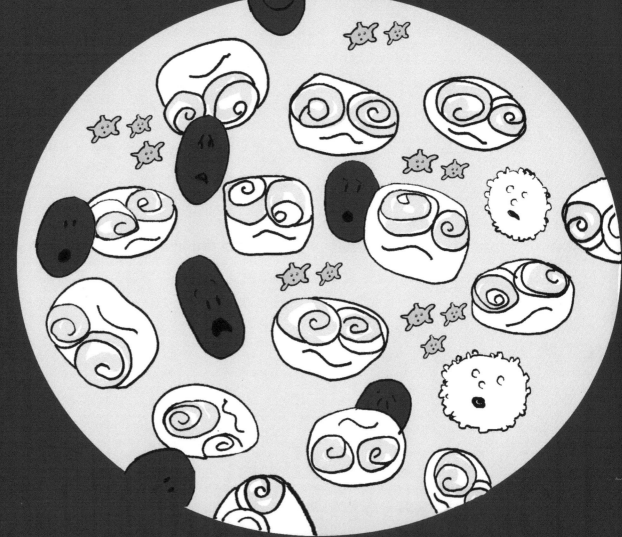

But my bone marrow couldn't stop making these cells. It made more and more. Soon there were so many of these lazy cells that there was no room left for the hard working cells.

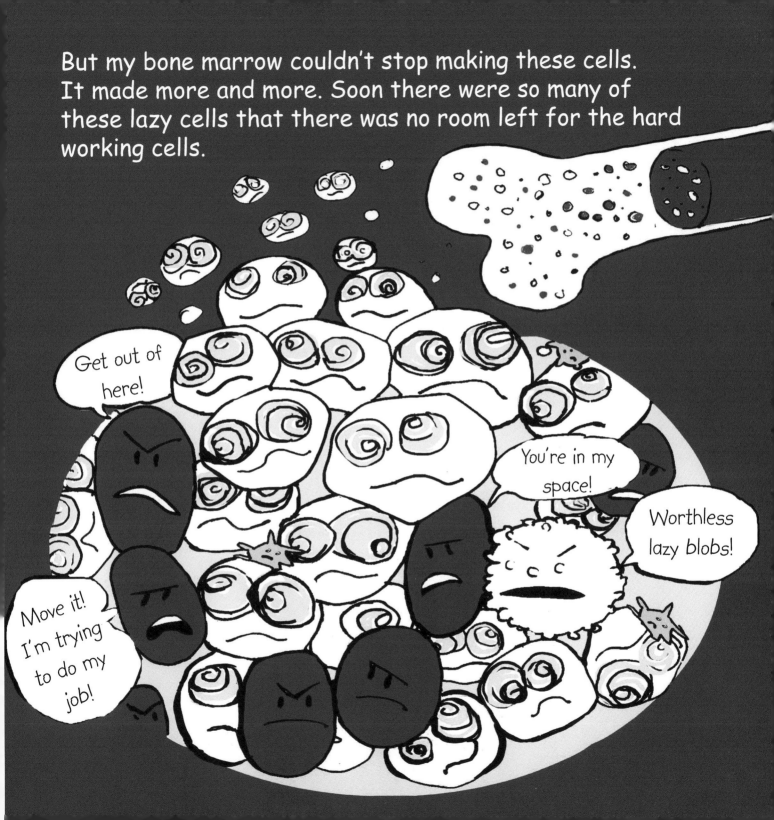

RED CELLS

Soon there were not enough red cells in my blood. I felt tired and breathless and my skin was pale.

WHITE CELLS

There were not enough white cells to eat the germs so I was getting sick often.

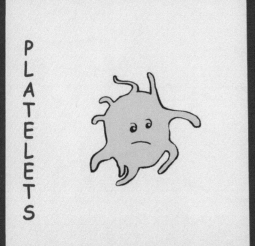

PLATELETS

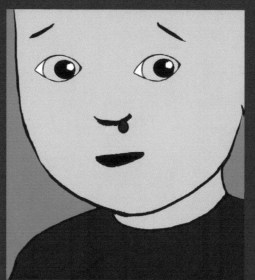

There were not enough platelets and I was bruising and bleeding more than usual. I needed help, FAST!

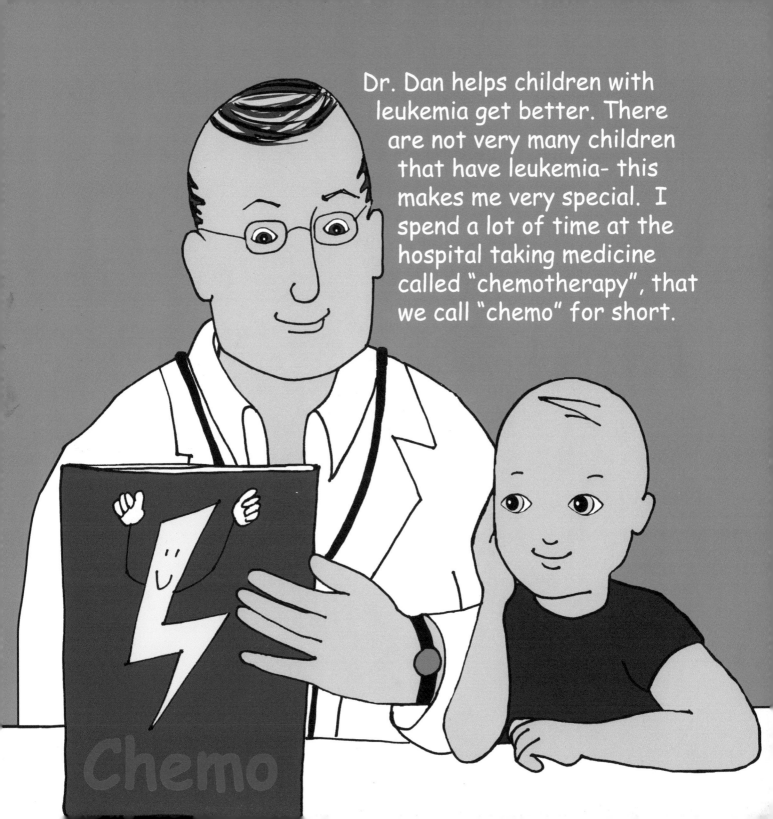

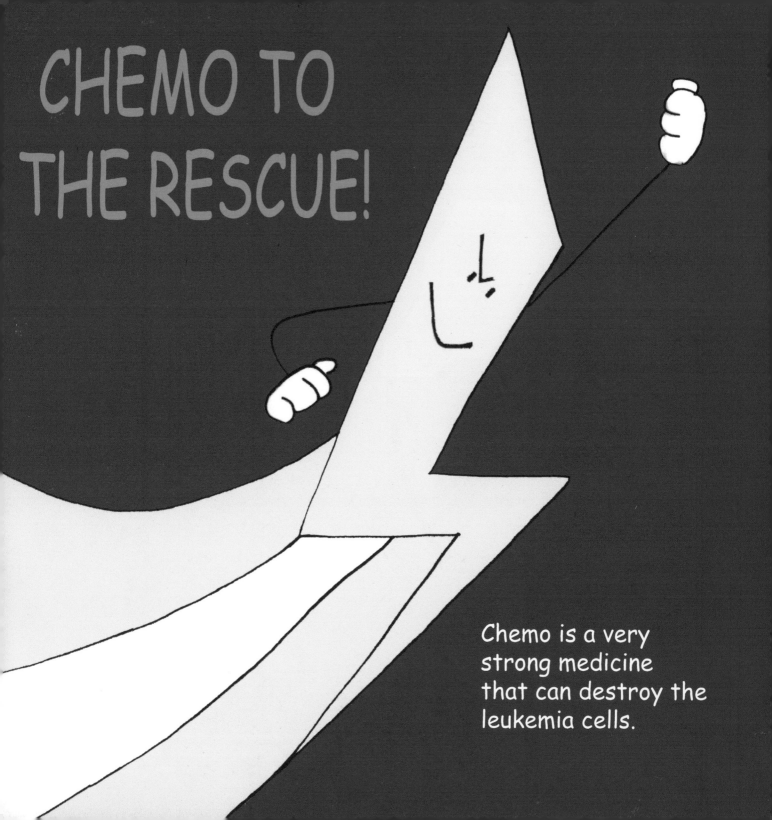

THERE ARE DIFFERENT WAYS OF TAKING CHEMO

Sometimes it is in pills.

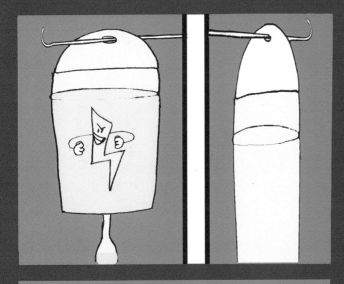

Sometimes it is in an IV.

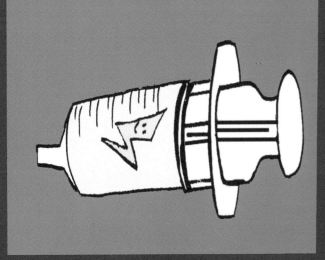

And sometimes it is in an injection.

ZAP! PING! POW!

Dr. Dan started my chemotherapy right away to destroy the leukemia.

WOW! It worked so well that...

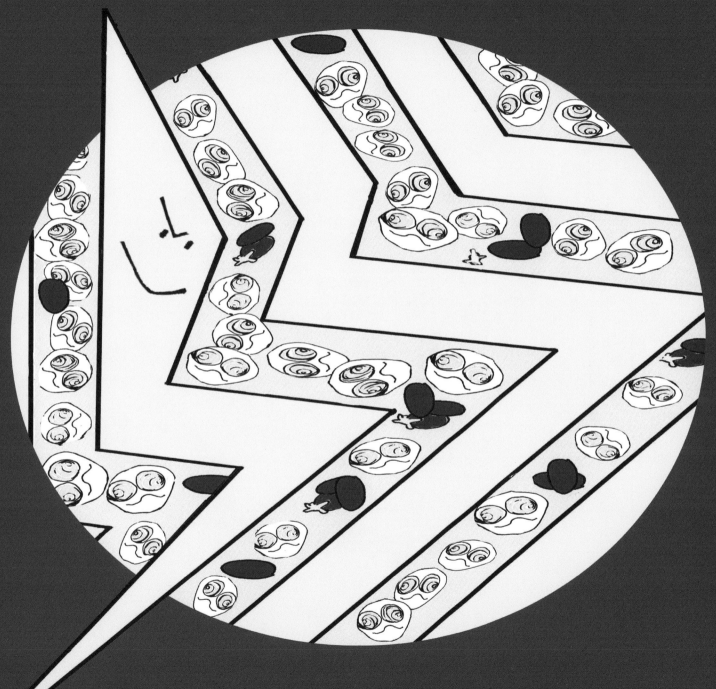

AT THE HOSPITAL

It is nice to have family here to take care of me.

I have met so many doctors and nurses. They are all very friendly, but sometimes I am a bit shy. They are working very hard to help me get better.

Before I start treatment I must put an "Emla" patch on. Emla is a magic cream that takes away the needle's sting.

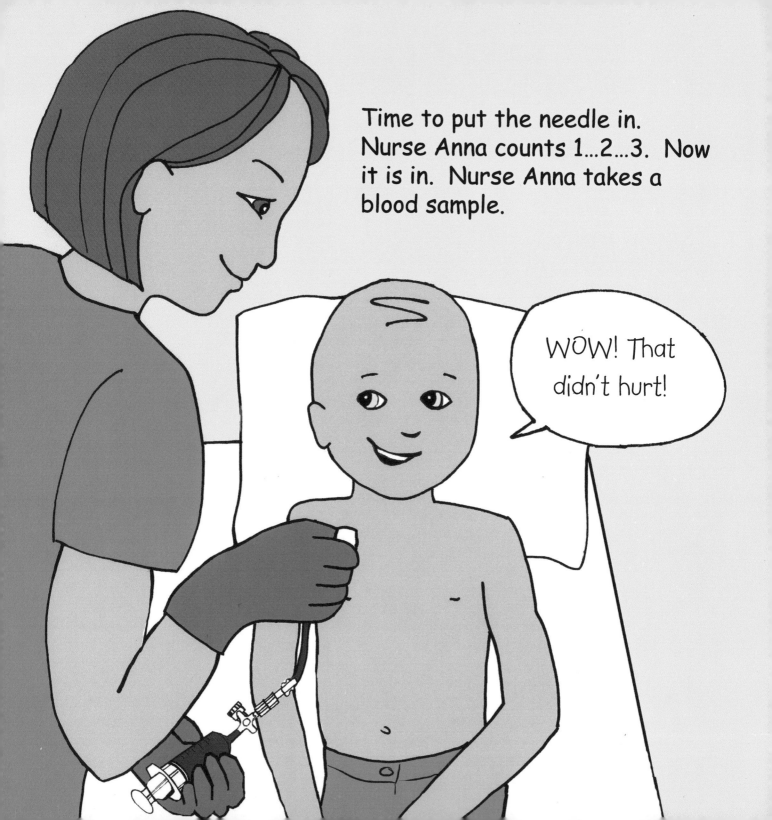

I'm high, I'm low,
I'm going through chemo.
No easy fight I know,
But I'm a superhero!
We'll make things right,
With chemo day and night.
Watch chemo zap it down,
And turn my life around!
Against my will,
I take another pill.
It's going to take some time,
Before I'm feeling fine.
Be brave! Be strong!
And take away what's wrong.
It's going to be alright,
The future's looking bright!

Chemotherapy affects rapidly dividing cells, even those found at the hair root. This is why my hair began to fall out about two weeks after my first treatment. It will grow back again one day, but for now, I started a collection of my favorite hats. My friend Emily likes to wear scarves.

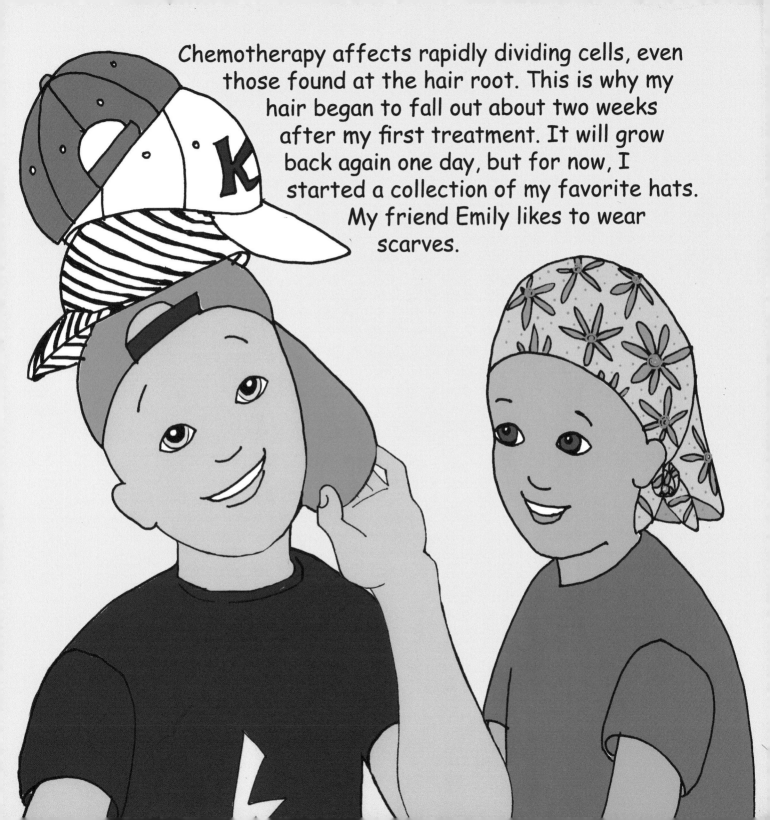

A
N
E
S
T
H
E
S
I
A

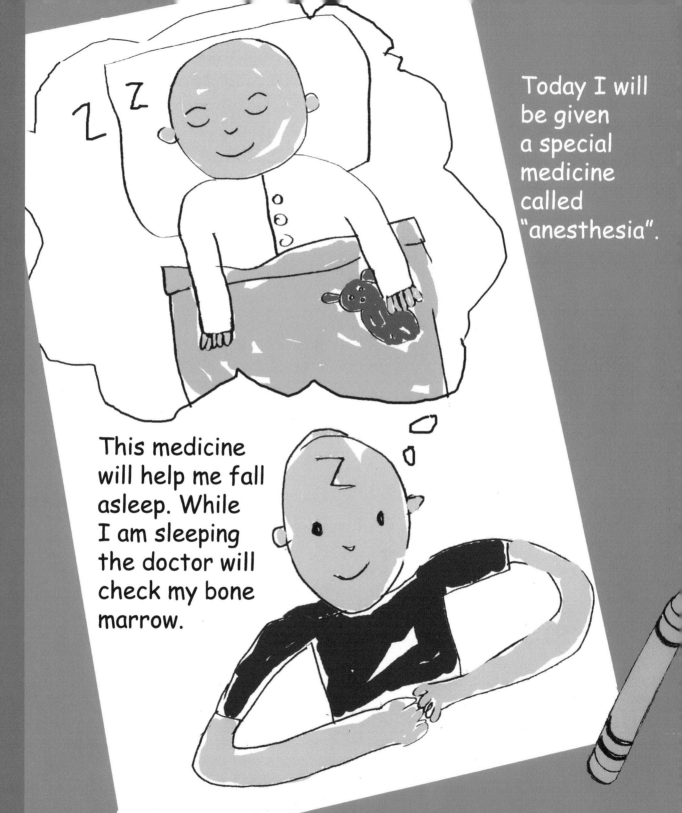

Today I will be given a special medicine called "anesthesia".

This medicine will help me fall asleep. While I am sleeping the doctor will check my bone marrow.

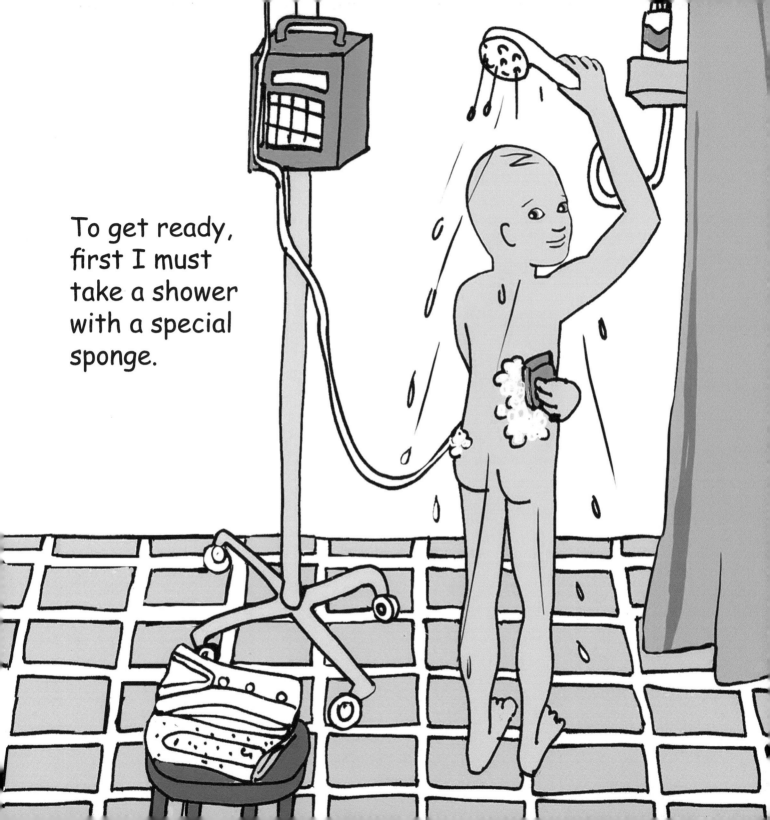

To get ready, first I must take a shower with a special sponge.

Then I put on
a clean white
hospital gown
with buttons
down the
front.

I can't eat or drink so I watch TV
to think about something else.

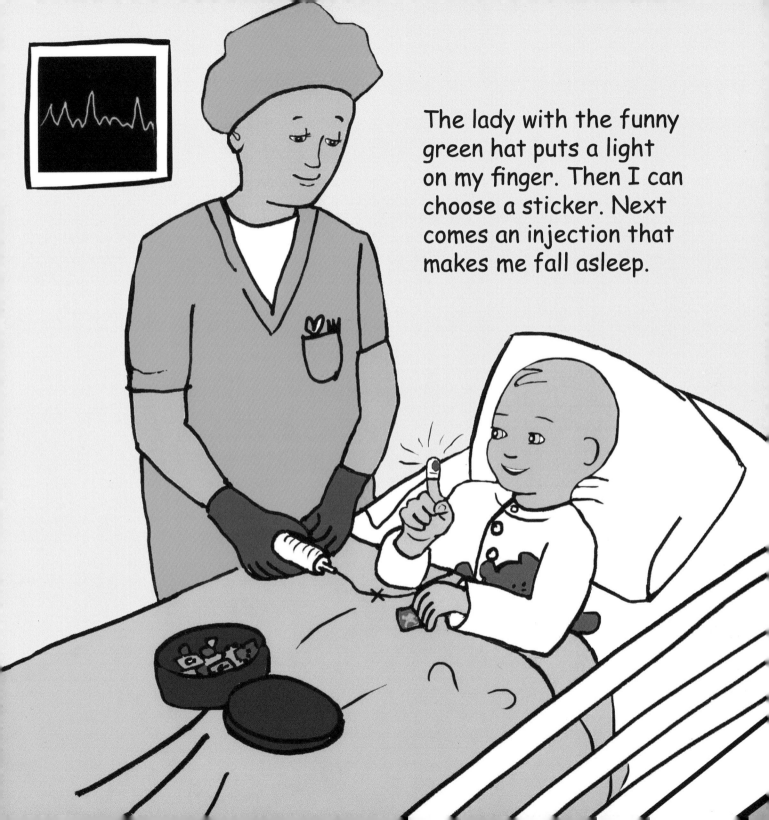

The lady with the funny green hat puts a light on my finger. Then I can choose a sticker. Next comes an injection that makes me fall asleep.

I count
1...2...3...4 and
then I fall
asleep, just
like that.

MEDICATION

Time to take a chemo pill. I put it on my tongue and float it down easy with lots of water. Down, down, down it goes into my stomach. Chemo goes to work right away.

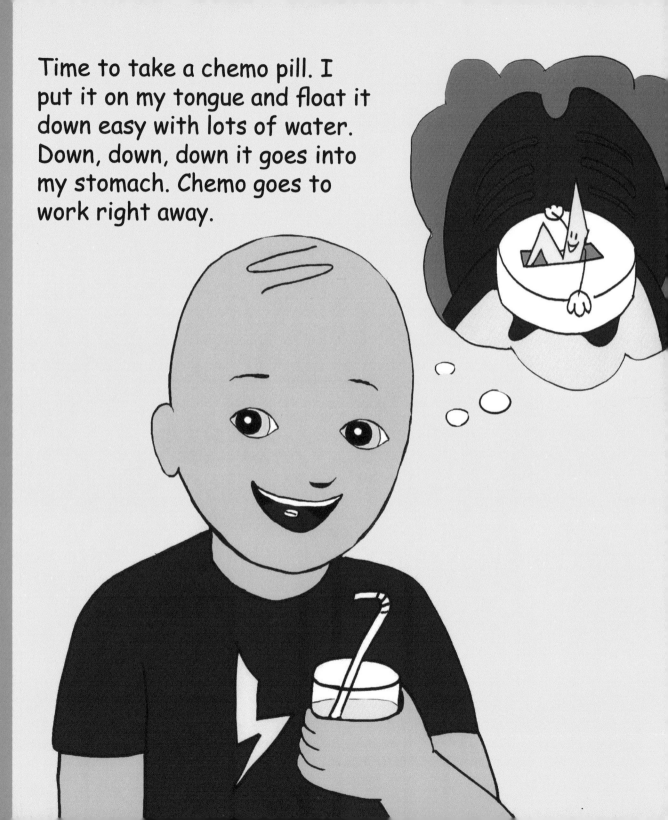

Some medicine can make me angry or sad for no reason. And some medicine can make me really hungry all the time. But it won't be long before I feel like myself again.

Unfortunately chemo takes away some of the good cells too. So now when I take a blood test Dr. Dan counts how many hard working cells there are in my blood.

BLOOD TEST

Can you count how many red blood cells there are in the picture? What would happen if you didn't have enough red blood cells? Now count the platelets. Do you remember what platelets do for your body? How many white cells do you see? What would happen if you have a low white blood count?

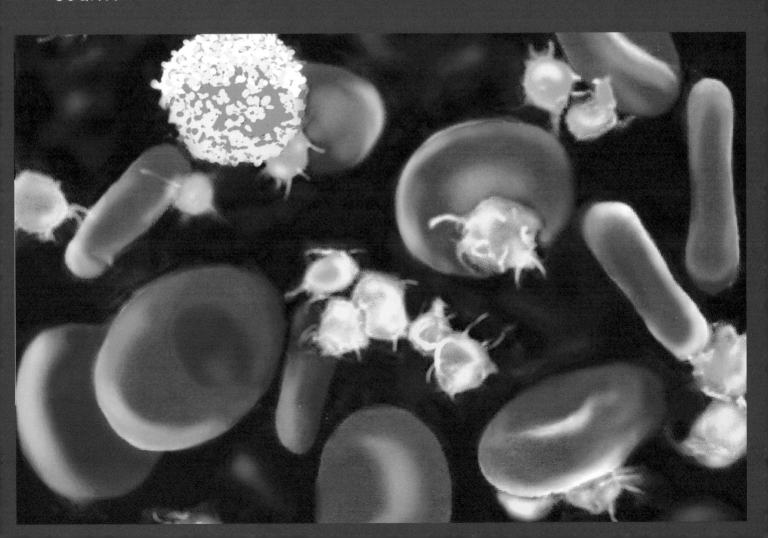

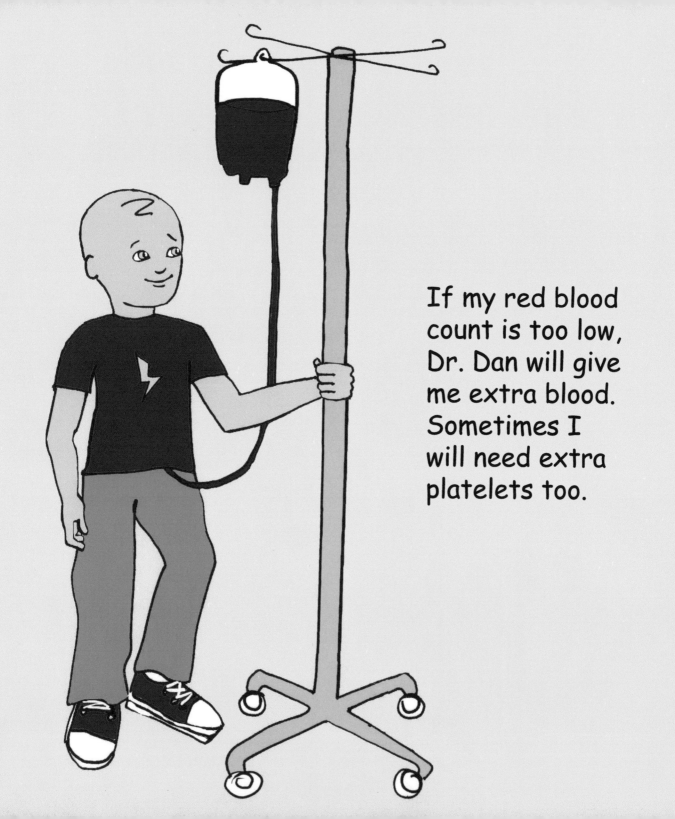

If my red blood
count is too low,
Dr. Dan will give
me extra blood.
Sometimes I
will need extra
platelets too.

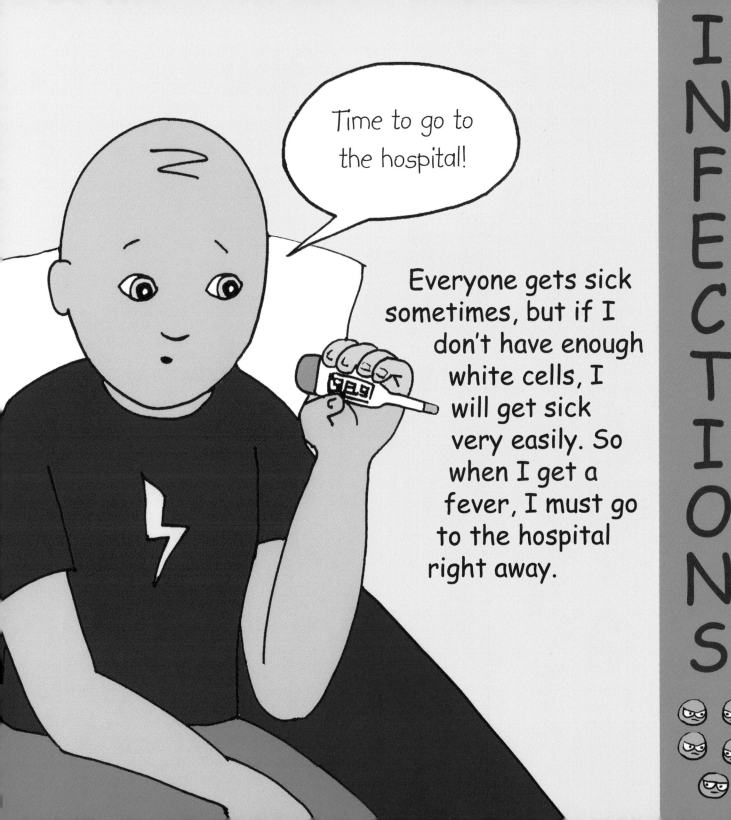

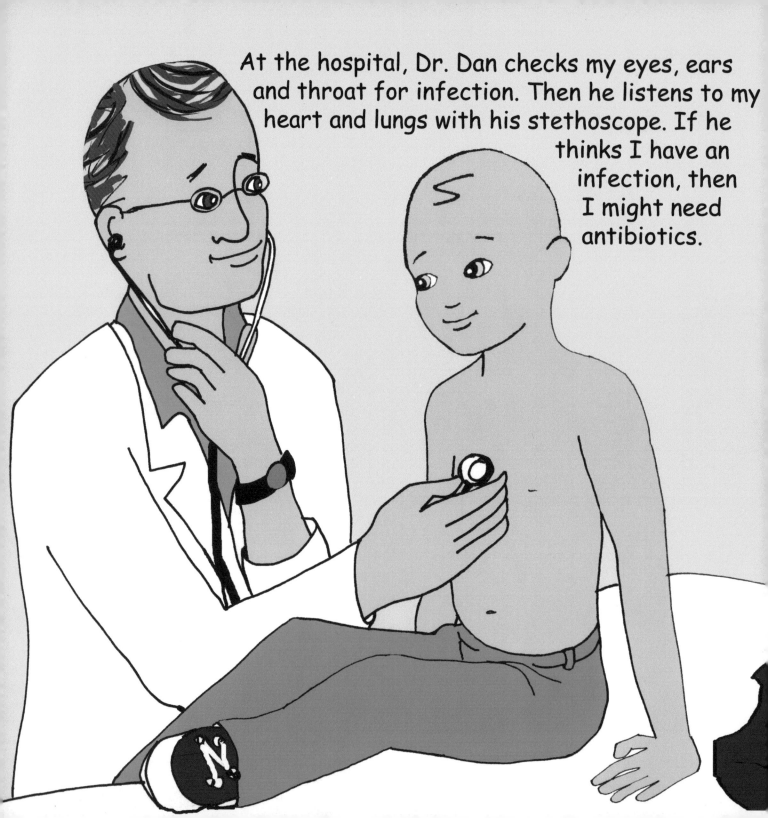

At the hospital, Dr. Dan checks my eyes, ears and throat for infection. Then he listens to my heart and lungs with his stethoscope. If he thinks I have an infection, then I might need antibiotics.

When I have an infection, my white cells might need extra help. Antibiotics are medicines that help the body fight infection.

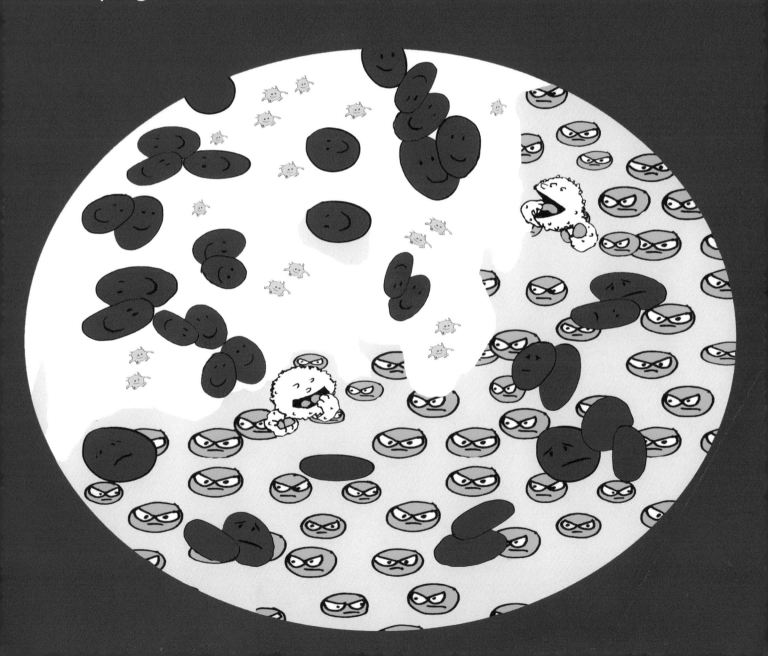

X RAYS

Sometimes I need x-rays. An x-ray machine can take a picture of what is inside my body. It can help the doctor find out fast if I have an infection and need antibiotics.

When my chemotherapy is finished, my body will be able to make lots of its own healthy blood cells again. Then I will feel strong again like before. One day I will look back on this time and think: WOW! I did it! And that is something to be proud of.